THE
ULTIMATE
GROSS
CHALLENGE

A BATTLE OF YUCKY CHOICES

JIMMY NIRO

sourcebooks
wonderland

Published by Sourcebooks Wonderland, and imprint of Sourcebooks Kids.
P.O. Box 4410, Naperville, Illinois 60567-4410
(630) 961-3900
sourcebookskids.com

This product conforms to all applicable CPSC and CPSIA standards.

Source of Production: Versa Press, East Peoria, Illinois, USA
Date of Production: August 2020
Run Number: 5019235

Printed and bound in the United States of America.
VP 10 9 8 7 6 5 4 3 2 1

CONTENTS

ARE YOU READY?

HOW TO PLAY

GOAL: Gross out your opponents and try to earn the most booger points!

How does it work?

Step 1: Find someone to play with! You can have just two players total or get a bunch of friends or family involved!

Step 2: Take turns reading the icky scenarios to each other.

Step 3: The player who has been read a gross or grosser scenario has to pick which one they would rather do. Remember, you can't answer neither! They also have to give a good explanation for why they would pick that option.

Step 4: Grab a pencil and a separate sheet of paper. Each gross option is ranked with booger points. When a player chooses an option and explains why, those points go toward their total booger score. Remember to keep track of the score as you go along!

Step 5: Read as many as you like! At the end, total up how many booger points each player earned to find out who's the **Booger Champion**!

How do you get started?

Play Rock Paper Scissors or flip a coin to decide who starts reading first.

And remember!

The nasty, disgusting, crazy, silly scenarios in this book are just for your imagination and having fun! **Please DON'T try any of these at home!**

GROSS OR GROSSER

PLAYER 1 STARTS READING HERE!

Could you have cockroaches fly out of your nose every time you sneezed?

BOOGER POINTS

OR

Would you have spiders crawl out of your eyes every time you cried?

BOOGER POINTS

Could you wear rotten fish-scented perfume for a week?

BOOGER POINTS

 OR

Would you prefer to have onion breath for a month?

BOOGER POINT

NOW TAKE TURNS READING AND
SCORING POINTS FOR THE
REST OF THE BOOK!

Could you eat a pizza with toenails as toppings?

BOOGER POINTS

OR

Would you eat a cupcake with earwax frosting?

BOOGER POINTS

Could you live with a pig nose for the rest of your life?

BOOGER POINTS

OR

Would you have a monkey tail for the rest of your life?

BOOGER POINTS

3

Could you eat a live fish?

OR

Would you take a bite of a dead snake?

EWW!

Could you drink a glass of lemonade with mayonnaise ice cubes?

BOOGER POINTS

OR

Would you prefer orange juice with ketchup ice cubes?

BOOGER POINT

Could you stand being covered with sticky glue for a week?

BOOGER POINT

OR

Would you prefer to be covered with itchy insect bites for a month?

BOOGER POINTS

Could you sleep in a stinky pigsty for a week?

BOOGER POINTS
✹ ✹ ✹

OR

Would you sleep in a smelly garbage bin for a week?

BOOGER POINTS
✹ ✹ ✹ ✹

- - - - - - - - - ✕ - - - - - - - - -

Could you stand farting every time you laughed?

BOOGER POINTS
✹ ✹

OR

Would you prefer burping every time you sat down?

BOOGER POINT
✹

Could you eat a handful of sand?

BOOGER POINTS

OR

Would you chew on a clump of someone else's hair?

BOOGER POINTS

Could you stand being ticklish over every inch of your body?

BOOGER POINT

OR

Would you prefer to always be shocked by static?

BOOGER POINTS

Could you stand having peanut butter stuck to the roof of your mouth for the rest of your life?

BOOGER POINTS

OR

Would you always have something stuck in your teeth for the rest of your life?

BOOGER POINT

Could you use a fridge that oozes green juice that smells like rotten eggs?

BOOGER POINTS

OR

Would you prefer to find rotten eggs in all of your pant pockets?

BOOGER POINTS

Could you eat an old potato chip you found between the cushions of a couch?

BOOGER POINTS

OR

Would you eat an old french fry you found on the floor of a car?

BOOGER POINTS

- - - - - - - - - - - - X - - - - - - - - - - - -

Could you stand burping uncontrollably in response to your friends talking to you?

BOOGER POINT

OR

Would you prefer if your friends burped in your face every time they ate lunch?

BOOGER POINTS

Could you stand always having the taste of garlic in your mouth?

 OR

Would you prefer sweating pickle juice for the rest of your life?

Could you lick the floor of your school cafeteria?

Would you prefer licking the toilet seat at home?

Could you stand having someone sneeze all over your hair?

BOOGER POINTS

Would you prefer having someone's blister burst on your face?

BOOGER POINTS

Could you stop showering for a month?

BOOGER POINTS

Would you prefer not changing your clothes for a month?

BOOGER POINTS

Could you write with every utensil you use always breaking?

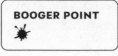

BOOGER POINT

Would you eat pencil shavings once?

BOOGER POINTS

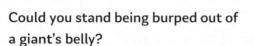

Could you stand being burped out of a giant's belly?

BOOGER POINTS

Would you prefer being sneezed out of a giant's nose?

BOOGER POINTS

14

Could you eat a donut filled with toe jam?

 OR

Would you eat a donut covered in belly button lint?

15

Could you lick a shopping cart whenever you went to the store?

BOOGER POINTS

OR

Would you prefer to sit on a wet seat whenever you were in a car?

BOOGER POINTS

Could you eat a strawberry-vomit pie?

BOOGER POINTS

OR

Would you drink a baby-poop smoothie?

BOOGER POINTS

Could you walk barefoot through a hallway covered in centipedes?

OR

Would you take a bath with live worms?

Could you eat only spinach for the rest of your life?

BOOGER POINT
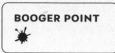

Would you blend all of your meals for the rest of your life?

BOOGER POINTS

Could you taste with your hands?

BOOGER POINTS

Would you prefer to smell with your feet?

BOOGER POINT

18

Could you keep dead animals that your cat drags in from outside in your room?

BOOGER POINTS

Would you prefer to have a pet tarantula that's allowed to roam your house uncaged?

BOOGER POINTS

Could you smell only dirty diapers for the rest of your life?

BOOGER POINTS

OR

Would you smell only sweaty armpits for the rest of your life?

BOOGER POINTS

Could you clean rain gutters by drinking the dirty water?

BOOGER POINTS

OR

Would you mow the lawn by eating grass?

BOOGER POINTS

Could you drink a glass of water from a dirty fish tank?

BOOGER POINTS

OR

Would you lick the liquid leaking from a garbage can?

BOOGER POINTS

Could you stand having warts cover your whole face for the rest of your life?

BOOGER POINTS

OR

Would you prefer having your whole face covered with hair?

BOOGER POINTS

- - - - - - - - - - - - ✕ - - - - - - - - - - - -

Could you stand having hair for teeth?

BOOGER POINTS

OR

Would you prefer having teeth for hair?

BOOGER POINTS

Could you clean a cat's litter box with your bare hands?

Would you lick a cat's butt?

Could you stand wearing someone's sweaty clothes for an hour?

BOOGER POINTS

Would you prefer smelling their socks for ten minutes?

BOOGER POINT

Could you eat a jar of mayonnaise with a spoon?

BOOGER POINTS
✹ ✹

OR

Would you drink a glass of old, moldy juice?

BOOGER POINTS
✹ ✹ ✹

- - - - - - - - - - - - - - ✕ - - - - - - - - - - - - - -

Could you stand wearing wet socks for a week?

BOOGER POINTS
✹ ✹

OR

Would you prefer to have popcorn kernels stuck in your teeth for a week?

BOOGER POINT
✹

Could you let spiders crawl in your hair for a day?

BOOGER POINTS

OR

Would you have ants in your socks for a day?

BOOGER POINTS

Could you use a dirty tube sock as a lunchbox?

BOOGER POINTS

OR

Would you use an unrinsed pickle jar as a water bottle?

BOOGER POINT

Could you lick off a stranger's eye crust?

BOOGER POINTS

OR

Would you lick your own toe jam?

BOOGER POINTS

27

Could you stick your head into a bucket of bacon fat?

BOOGER POINTS

 OR

Would you put your hand into a tank of live rats?

BOOGER POINTS

Could you go a day with raw eggs in your underwear?

BOOGER POINTS

OR

Would you spend a day with mashed potatoes in your shoes?

BOOGER POINT

Could you use anchovy-flavored toothpaste?

BOOGER POINTS

OR

Would you floss your teeth with someone's back hair?

BOOGER POINTS

Could you chew the gum stuck to the bottom of your desk?

BOOGER POINTS

OR

Would you wear underwear from the school's lost and found?

BOOGER POINTS

Could you clean up someone else's vomit with your hands?

BOOGER POINTS

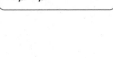
OR

Would you prefer to gag whenever you took a bite of food?

BOOGER POINT

Could you use a towel you found on the ground outside?

BOOGER POINTS

Would you use a hairbrush you found in the dumpster?

BOOGER POINTS

Could you rinse your mouth with broccoli mouthwash?

BOOGER POINT

 OR

Would you wash your face with toilet water?

BOOGER POINTS

Could you hold a moth in your mouth for five seconds?

BOOGER POINTS

OR

Would you hold an eel in your hands for five minutes?

BOOGER POINTS

Could you eat an entire bag of dead flies?

BOOGER POINTS

OR

Would you prefer having live flies come out of your mouth every time you coughed for the next year?

BOOGER POINTS

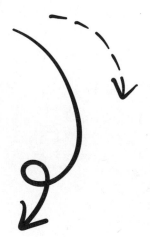

Could you wash stinky dishes with your tongue?

BOOGER POINTS

OR

Would you separate dirty laundry with your teeth?

BOOGER POINTS

Could you sleep with sheets made of bologna?

BOOGER POINTS

OR

Would you wear clothes made of slimy seaweed?

BOOGER POINTS

Could you stand falling into a pit of clipped toenails?

BOOGER POINTS

OR

Would you prefer to be inside a porta potty when it fell over?

BOOGER POINTS

Could you stand having sweat glands in your mouth?

BOOGER POINTS

OR

Would you prefer having taste buds on your butt?

BOOGER POINTS

Could you stand having octopus tentacles for hair?

BOOGER POINTS

OR

Would you prefer having porcupine spikes for fingernails?

BOOGER POINTS

Could you say hello to people by sniffing their butts?

BOOGER POINTS

OR

Would you say goodbye by licking earlobes?

BOOGER POINTS

Could you use a litter box as a bathroom for a month?

BOOGER POINTS

OR

Would you eat and drink out of a dog bowl for a year?

BOOGER POINTS

Could you stand constantly drooling for the rest of your life?

BOOGER POINTS

OR

Would you prefer having a runny nose for the rest of your life?

BOOGER POINTS

Could you eat cheese that smelled like stinky socks?

BOOGER POINTS

Would you wear socks that smelled like stinky cheese for a whole week?

BOOGER POINTS

Could you sleep on a pillow covered with drool?

BOOGER POINTS

Would you sleep on a pillow covered in swamp water?

BOOGER POINTS

- - - - - - - - - - ✕ - - - - - - - - - -

Could you collect rotten eggs?

BOOGER POINTS

Would you keep a beehive in your bedroom?

BOOGER POINTS

Could you pee sand for the rest of your life?

OR

Would you eat a pine cone every day for the rest of your life?

Could you pop someone's pimple?

 OR

Would you let a stranger pop your pimple?

Could you serve your family a road-kill meatloaf?

 OR

Would you eat it yourself so they wouldn't have to?

Could you drink a smoothie of ground guts?

BOOGER POINTS

OR

Would you wear earwax lip balm?

BOOGER POINTS

Could you sprinkle dandruff flakes onto your food?

BOOGER POINTS

OR

Would you sprinkle floor sweepings instead?

BOOGER POINTS

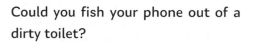

Could you fish your phone out of a dirty toilet?

BOOGER POINTS

OR

Would you use your toothbrush to clean the dirty toilet?

BOOGER POINTS

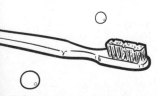

Could you eat chocolate that tasted like poop?

Would you eat poop that tasted like chocolate?

Could you live in a sewer?

BOOGER POINTS

Would you live in the desert while wearing two sweaters and two pairs of pants?

BOOGER POINTS

Could you stand having flaps of skin dangling from your elbows?

BOOGER POINTS

OR

Would you prefer having extra teeth in your nostrils?

BOOGER POINTS

Could you eat off a toilet seat?

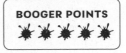

OR

Would you eat off the bottom of a sewer plate?

Could you eat a grasshopper?

BOOGER POINTS

 OR

Would you lick a dung beetle?

BOOGER POINTS

Could you walk through a hallway of raw eggs?

 OR

Would you let fish nibble dead skin off your feet?

Could you eat moldy cauliflower?

 OR

Would you eat stinky, expired sauerkraut?

Could you stick a gooey booger in your ear?

BOOGER POINTS

OR

Would you put earwax in your nose?

BOOGER POINTS

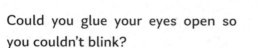

Could you glue your eyes open so you couldn't blink?

BOOGER POINTS

OR

Would you glue your mouth open so bugs could fly in?

BOOGER POINTS

Could you drink a glass of milk through your nose?

OR

Would you drink a glass of hot sauce?

Could you use toilet paper made of dirty leaves?

Would you use eye drops made of lemon juice?

Could you chew soap-flavored gum?

OR

Would you prefer brussels sprout-flavored gum?

Could you make oatmeal in the toilet bowl and eat it?

Would you eat noodles boiled in vomit?

Could you stand having tongues for fingers?

BOOGER POINTS

OR

Would you prefer having toes for teeth?

BOOGER POINTS

Could you eat kitty litter?

BOOGER POINTS

OR

Would you rather step in dog pee while wearing only socks?

BOOGER POINTS

Could you sleep on a pillow made of eyeballs?

BOOGER POINTS

Would you snuggle up in a blanket full of fish guts?

BOOGER POINTS

Could you put a live bug in your ear?

BOOGER POINTS

OR

Would you put a live bug in your pants?

BOOGER POINTS

Could you always use the same dirty spoon to eat?

BOOGER POINTS

OR

Would you prefer to only eat with your hands?

BOOGER POINT

Could you eat a bowl full of scabs?

BOOGER POINTS

 OR

Would you prefer a bowl full of ants?

BOOGER POINTS

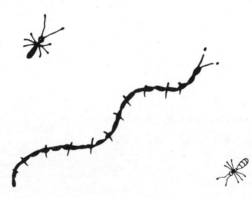

Could you stand in the rain if it were pouring snail slime?

BOOGER POINTS

 OR

Would you stand in a blizzard of yellow snow?

BOOGER POINTS

Could you stand having someone chew your food before you ate it?

BOOGER POINTS

OR

Would you prefer drinking only backwash?

BOOGER POINTS

Could you eat a fart?

 OR

Would you prefer getting sprayed in the face by a skunk?

Could you hug a zombie?

BOOGER POINTS

OR

Would you kiss a goblin?

BOOGER POINTS

Could you live with a belly button the size of a cinnamon roll?

BOOGER POINTS

OR

Would you prefer to have extra-long armpit hair that stuck out of your shirtsleeve?

BOOGER POINTS

Could you eat the food that someone picked from between their teeth?

BOOGER POINTS

OR

Would you lick melted ice cream off a hot sidewalk?

BOOGER POINTS

Could you stand having bloody sores all around your mouth for the rest of your life?

BOOGER POINTS

OR

Would you prefer to have flaky chapped lips for the rest of your life?

BOOGER POINT

Could you chew gum that your friend had just chewed?

BOOGER POINTS

OR

Would you listen to someone pop their gum right by your ear for an hour straight?

BOOGER POINTS

Could you use motor oil as shampoo?

Would you use ranch dressing as body wash?

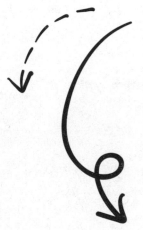

Could you stand having every baby you ever held spit up on you?

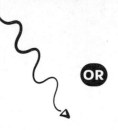

OR

Would you have every toddler you passed cough in your face?

Could you stand having fish scales for skin?

OR

Would you prefer having dog fur all over your body?

Could you stick your hand in a barrel of cow tongues?

Would you prefer if every person in your class touched your tongue once?

Could you stand your phone screen feeling greasy whenever you touched it?

BOOGER POINTS

OR

Would you prefer using a keyboard that made fart noises whenever you typed?

BOOGER POINT

Could you listen to someone vomiting on loop whenever you listened to music?

BOOGER POINTS

OR

Would you prefer to vomit every time you tried to sing?

BOOGER POINTS

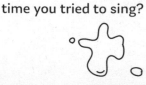

66

Could you stand having lice for a month?

BOOGER POINTS

OR

Would you prefer having a poison ivy rash for a year?

BOOGER POINTS

Could you dump trash on your couch before you sat on it?

OR

Would you put a used toilet plunger on your bed before you went to sleep?

Could you live with always having sticky hands?

OR

Would you prefer having your tongue feel prickly?

Could you eat food off a stranger's used plate?

BOOGER POINT

OR

Would you prefer to find someone else's hair on your plate?

BOOGER POINTS

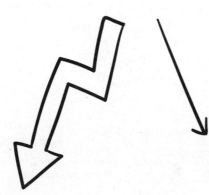

Could you throw up hairballs like a
cat every time you coughed?

BOOGER POINTS
✹ ✹ ✹

OR

Would you prefer to drool like a dog
every time you felt hungry?

BOOGER POINTS
✹ ✹

YUCK!

Could you swallow your snot for a month?

OR

Would you use the same small tissue for a month?

Could you braid your dad's sweaty armpit hairs?

OR

Would lick your own hand every time someone gave you a handshake?

Could you drink a glass of spoiled chocolate milk?

BOOGER POINTS

Would you eat unwrapped food that fell on the bathroom floor?

BOOGER POINTS

Could you drink a glass of salt water with every meal?

OR

Would you have all of your food pre-pared with hot dog juice?

- - - - - - - - - - - - X - - - - - - - - - - - -

Could you wear the same pair of underwear for a month?

OR

Would you wear your grandma's smelliest perfume for a month?

Could you wear your friend's dirty retainer?

Would you wear your own retainer after you dropped in the trash?

- - - - - - - - - - X - - - - - - - - - - -

Could you listen to someone scratch their nails on the chalkboard at the beginning of every class?

Would you eat all of the chalk in the classroom?

Could you stand having sandpaper for hands?

BOOGER POINTS

OR

Would you prefer having dirty sponges for feet?

BOOGER POINTS

Could you use lotion that smelled like rotten fish?

BOOGER POINTS

OR

Would you spray your room with fart spray?

BOOGER POINTS

Could you change a baby's stinky diaper in the dark?

BOOGER POINTS

OR

Would you clean up dog poop from your yard at night while barefoot?

BOOGER POINTS

Could you lick a bandage you found
on the ground?

Would you wear someone else's used
bandage as your own?

Could you eat all liquids as solids for the rest of your life?

BOOGER POINTS
✳ ✳ ✳

OR

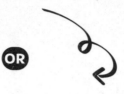

Would you drink all solids as liquids for the rest of your life?

BOOGER POINTS
✳ ✳

Could you drink a glass of sweat?

BOOGER POINTS
✳ ✳ ✳ ✳ ✳

OR

Would you drink your sibling's bath water?

BOOGER POINTS
✳ ✳ ✳ ✳

Could you eat cow manure?

BOOGER POINTS

Would you eat a dead spider off the floor?

BOOGER POINTS

Could you eat four sticks of butter?

BOOGER POINTS
✹ ✹ ✹

OR

Would you eat a small bar of soap?

BOOGER POINTS
✹ ✹ ✹

Could you stand having foot-long eyebrow hair?

BOOGER POINTS
✹ ✹

OR

Would you prefer having a boil the size of a golf ball on your forehead?

BOOGER POINTS
✹ ✹ ✹

Could you bite into a piece of candy filled with pus?

 OR

Would you bite into a burrito filled with beetles?

Could you stand smelling like poop for the rest of your life if you weren't able to smell yourself?

Would you prefer if every person you lived with for the rest of your life smelled like poop?

Could you stand finding a dead rat in the fridge every time you opened it?

Would you prefer to hear rats in the walls every time you tried to sleep?

Could you drink a cup of a stranger's saliva?

BOOGER POINTS

Would you prefer to eat all the hair from their bathtub drain?

BOOGER POINTS

Could you chew on a mouthful of your own fingernails?

BOOGER POINTS
✹ ✹ ✹

Would you chew on a mouthful of your own toe jam?

BOOGER POINTS
✹ ✹ ✹ ✹

Could you stand being given a fart in a jar for every birthday as a present?

BOOGER POINTS

OR

Would you prefer to eat a birthday cake frosted with toothpaste for every birthday?

BOOGER POINTS

Could you stand having your tongue always feel slimy?

BOOGER POINTS

OR

Would you prefer having breath that smelled like rotten meat for the rest of your life?

BOOGER POINTS

Could you stand having your throat coated with mucus for the rest of your life?

BOOGER POINTS

 OR

Would you prefer to have your ears overflow with earwax for the rest of your life?

BOOGER POINTS

- - - - - - - - - X - - - - - - - -

Could you wear clothes that always smelled like moth balls?

BOOGER POINT

 OR

Would you prefer to wash all of your clothes in spoiled milk?

BOOGER POINTS

Could you stand finding ticks in your fridge?

BOOGER POINTS
✳ ✳ ✳ ✳

OR

Would you prefer to find a family of possums in your closet?

BOOGER POINTS
✳ ✳ ✳

Could you add frosting to all of your sandwiches?

OR

Would you put spicy peppers on all of your desserts?

Could you use bodywash made of soy sauce?

BOOGER POINTS

Would you use lotion that made you smell like vinegar?

BOOGER POINTS

Could you gargle barbecue sauce?

BOOGER POINTS

Would you eat fish food as a condiment?

BOOGER POINTS

Could you let a beetle live under your skin for a day?

Would you let a mouse sleep in your mouth overnight?

Could you stand it if everyone around you slurped while they drank?

BOOGER POINTS

Would you prefer having everyone around you chew with their mouths open?

BOOGER POINT

Could you have all the floors in your house carpeted with human hair?

BOOGER POINTS

OR

Would you use a blanket that always smells like a cat peed on it?

BOOGER POINTS

Could you wear your friend's sweaty socks all day after gym class?

BOOGER POINTS

OR

Would you prefer to find your back-pack filled with sweaty socks?

BOOGER POINT

- - - - - - - - - ✕ - - - - - - - - -

Could you suck milk straight from a cow's udder?

BOOGER POINTS

OR

Would you eat a deep-fried tarantula?

BOOGER POINTS

Could you drink one-hundred-year-old eggnog?

 OR

Would you eat a gingerbread house frosted with shaving cream?

YUCK!

Could you stand to have everything you eat taste like black licorice for a year?

BOOGER POINTS

Would you have everything you drink smell like gasoline for a year?

BOOGER POINTS

- - - - - - - - - - - - ✕ - - - - - - - - - - - -

Could you pick the scabs off a stranger's back?

BOOGER POINTS

Would you use someone's dandruff as baby powder?

BOOGER POINTS

Could you eat baby snakes as pasta?

BOOGER POINTS

OR

Would you eat dish sponges as sand-wich bread?

BOOGER POINTS

Could you live in a house with walls made out of dead frogs for a week?

BOOGER POINTS

OR

Would you ride in a car filled with flying bats?

BOOGER POINTS

Could you stand to have baby hands?

BOOGER POINTS

OR

Would you prefer to have clown feet?

BOOGER POINT

Could you snuggle a wet dog covered in mud?

BOOGER POINTS

OR

Would you sit next to a kid on the bus who won't stop farting?

BOOGER POINTS

Could you let people wipe their snot on your sleeve whenever they cried?

BOOGER POINTS

OR

Would you pick your nose every time you asked a question?

BOOGER POINTS

Could you stand peeing a little every time you blinked?

BOOGER POINT

OR

Would you prefer puking a little every time someone said your name?

BOOGER POINTS

Could you stand hearing a squelch every time you took a step?

 OR

Would you prefer having to chew everything you drink?

Could you live with being named "Phlegm"?

BOOGER POINTS

OR

Would you call your teacher "Mom" for a year?

BOOGER POINTS

Could you wear the same Halloween costume to school for a month without washing it?

BOOGER POINTS

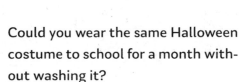

OR

Would you wear a jacket made of raw chicken skin for an hour?

BOOGER POINTS

Could you stand sweating salad dressing?

OR

Would you prefer to cry hot sauce?

Could you drink chunky, curdled milk?

Would you drink a buffalo-snot milkshake?

Could you drink orange juice every morning after brushing your teeth?

BOOGER POINT

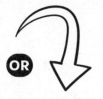

OR

Would you brush your teeth with someone else's finger?

BOOGER POINTS

Could you lick the floor of a school bus?

BOOGER POINTS

OR

Would you clean out a hamster cage using only your hands?

BOOGER POINTS

Could you listen to brakes squealing every time you tried to sleep?

BOOGER POINTS

OR

Would you have a baby's screams as an alarm clock?

BOOGER POINT

Could you stand being drenched with sweat all day but not smell?

BOOGER POINTS

OR

Would you prefer having hair suddenly grow on random parts of your body?

BOOGER POINT

Could you let a dog give you kisses after it just cleaned its butt?

Would you let your mom give you a big kiss and tell you what a good kid you are in front of your entire school?

Could you use an extremely dirty public toilet in the dark?

BOOGER POINTS

OR

Would you use a toilet with a snake in it?

BOOGER POINTS

Could you share a scrub brush with a raccoon?

BOOGER POINTS

OR

Would you use a scratchy blanket that always gives you a rash?

BOOGER POINT

Could you shower with sewage water?

BOOGER POINTS

OR

Would you prefer having sidewalk gum stuck in your hair for a week?

BOOGER POINTS

Could you eat toast with liver spread?

OR

Would you eat a hamburger with cat food on it?

Could you live with a condition that made you sneeze one thousand times a day?

OR

Would you prefer to live with a condition that made you pee your pants in public once a year?

Could you touch your eyeball with dirty fingers?

BOOGER POINTS
✹ ✹ ✹

 OR

Would you lick a stranger's nose?

BOOGER POINTS
✹ ✹ ✹ ✹

Could you stand walking into a spider web every time you went outside?

BOOGER POINTS

OR

Would you prefer to have a bird poop on your head whenever you walked outside?

BOOGER POINTS

- - - - - - - - - - - - - - X - - - - - - - - - - - -

Could you use a TV remote with only your tongue?

BOOGER POINTS

OR

Would you prefer if everyone only used their bare toes when using your video game controllers?

BOOGER POINT

Could you pull rotting food out of a clogged kitchen sink?

BOOGER POINTS

OR

Would you prefer to find random clumps of human hair in your house?

BOOGER POINTS

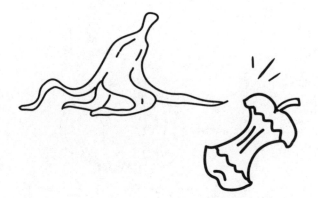

Could you sit through a movie with someone who smelled like garlic sitting next to you?

BOOGER POINTS

OR

Would you eat old popcorn off the dirty floor of the theater?

BOOGER POINTS

WHO'S THE BOOGER CHAMPION?

Count up how many booger points each player or team earned, and write the totals to find out who's the champion!

PLAYER 1 TOTAL WINS _____

PLAYER 2 TOTAL WINS _____

_____

_____

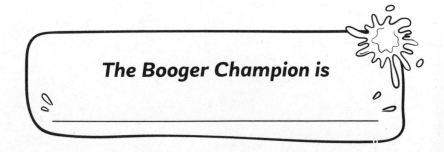

The Booger Champion is

_____

GROSS-OUT
HALL OF FAME

Write down the weirdest and wackiest scenarios from the book, and save them for when you really want to gross out another player!

350+ SILLY, LAUGH-OUT-LOUD JOKES FOR THE WHOLE FAMILY!

DAD JOKES FOR KIDS!

THEY'RE DINO-MITE!

JIMMY NIRO

DAD JOKES

the GOOD.
the BAD.
the TERRIBLE.

- Jimmy Niro

JIMMY NIRO

DAD JOKES

HOLIDAY EDITION!

YULE LOVE THEM!

SUPER!!!

DAD JOKES

SAVING THE WORLD, ONE BAD JOKE AT A TIME

JIMMY NIRO